ENGLISH COSTUME OF
THE LATER MIDDLE AGES

English Costume

of the

Later Middle Ages

The Fourteenth and Fifteenth Centuries

Drawn and described by

IRIS BROOKE

Adam and Charles Black

FIRST PUBLISHED 1935
REPRINTED 1948, 1956, 1963, 1970, 1977

A. & C. BLACK LTD
35 BEDFORD ROW, LONDON WC1R 4JH
© A. & C. BLACK LTD

ISBN 0 7136 0155 8

PRINTED IN GREAT BRITAIN BY TINDAL PRESS LTD.

1300

FOREWORD

AS in the previous books in this series, my aim has been
to select interesting and popular garments, head-
dresses, footwear, and details of costume of the period.
It is not easy in the limited space available to depict the
progress of costume during two centuries, and inevitably
there are omissions. A great deal of time and thought,
however, has been expended on a selection of drawings
which will give a maximum of information to the student
with limited hours at his disposal and only a slight knowledge
of costume.

If the costume of a period is, as Mr. James Laver sug-
gests, the mirror of the soul, there are several interesting
reflections in the costume of the fourteenth and fifteenth
centuries. The contrast between the dress of the noble and
that of the labourer is more striking than at any later period
in English history, and it indicates the distinction which the
feudal system demanded between the powerful baron and
the powerless serf. With the gradual decay of this system
later in the fourteenth century, class distinction in dress
began a slow process of disintegration which ended only in
recent times. Changes in costume were few in the early
years of the century, but with the achievement of national
unity—the complete fusion of the Norman conquerors and
the Anglo-Saxon conquered, and the progress of national
freedom in the increasing powers of Parliament—English
life showed fresh strength and vigour, which is reflected to a
remarkable extent in the costume of the latter half of the
fourteenth century. Clothes assumed a new importance,
and new and exaggerated fashions made great headway.
It was with the arrival of Anne of Bohemia in the 'eighties
that the most fantastic and exaggerated fashions made their
appearance, and from this time onwards until the Puritan

influence of the seventeenth century, costume became more and more ornate. The exaggeration of each phase of fashion beyond the point of absurdity seems to have been the aim of every would-be " Elligant " of the fifteenth century.

The new virility and gladness of English life which found utterance in the verse of Chaucer and his *Tales of the Canterbury Pilgrim* seem to have died with him, but in the century which followed, in spite of the wars with France and the Wars of the Roses, the gay progress of costume continued, and both men and women found ample opportunity for self-expression in dress. Costumes were still fantastic and exaggerated when the acquisition of wealth and material prosperity under the Tudors permitted still further elaboration, so that the fifteenth century closes and the age of Elizabeth opens with pageantry more lavish than at any other period in the history of English costume.

I. B.

1300—1325

CLOTHES worn during the first quarter of the fourteenth century were a motley of a dozen countries. It was a time when England sought and found inspiration for costumes, manners, and furnishings from the Continent and from the East.

It is impossible at this early date to talk of fashion, as we understand the word. Cloth was both expensive and enduring, and one well-woven garment might serve three generations, its usefulness not diminishing with age. Elementary ideas of personal and domestic cleanliness prevailed, and there was a constant struggle against famine and disease. The wars with Scotland and France, and the strife between the Crown and the Barony, left little time for the consideration of dress apart from its utility.

This tendency to severe utility is well illustrated by the two costumes in the frontispiece. These simple loosely-fitting garments, almost devoid of ornament, are typical of thousands that might have been seen in the early years of the fourteenth century.

There is so little change in clothes, and so little variety, in the early period of this century, that one page of sketches is almost enough to show the foundation of practically every type of garment. A man of nobility and wealth wore furs and velvets, and his gowns were usually voluminous and all-enveloping. The women wore a tight-fitting garment, which we will call a kirtle to distinguish it from the outer gown, and over it a surcoat. This garment was split at the sides, and, being sleeveless, displayed the sleeves of the undergarment. A girdle or belt, with pouch attached, was worn either at the waist or a little lower, but little attention was paid to finishing touches. Aprons were worn to a great extent by the people; with this exception, the costume illustrated might be that of a lady of quality. The jester at this time was an important personage in every large household. Later in the century his traditional dress became much more elaborate.

1 3 0 0—1 3 2 5 *(continued)*

The coif, a close-fitting bonnet tied under the chin, which enclosed the hair and ears, was worn extensively by men ; over this the hat or bonnet was worn. The heads of both men and women inclined to drapery rather than to any formality in headdress. Men wore their hair long—almost to the shoulders. Women always parted their hair in the centre, and wore it in plaits doubled over the ears or confined in a chignon or net. The nets were often ornamented with beads or gilt spangles. In some contemporary drawings the hair is shown in a loose plait or twist hanging down the back.

As the hood, with its gorget and liripipe, became the foundation for dozens of head-arrangements throughout the fourteenth century and the first half of the fifteenth century, it is perhaps advisable, at this stage, to explain how this fantastic fashion began. At first the hood was merely a cowl with a point at the back, with a gorget hanging down over the shoulders. In the next stage the point at the back of the hood was elongated, often to an absurd length, by the addition of a long pipe of the material, or a " liripipe," as it was called. The lengthening of this appendage and the ornamentation of the edge of the gorget were seized on with delight and elaborated to ridiculous extremes by the dandies of the period.

In the early years of the fourteenth century the opening in the hood, which had been previously left for the face, was placed on the head, and the gorget then fell like a scarf from the side or the top of the head, on to one shoulder, and the liripipe on to the other. Later, the liripipe was wound round the head, and the gorget with its jagged edges stood out like a cockscomb. The front part of the facial opening was rolled back to form a brim, and during the fifteenth century this was stiffened, and the liripipe became a wide scarf which was often draped round the chin. The slow evolution of headgear from a simple cowl to the absurdly fantastic head-dresses of the fifteenth century can be traced with ease in the following pages.

1325—1350

THE two costumes illustrated here, of about 1340, have assumed a definite cut and shape which previously had been lacking in both men's and women's attire. The figure-fitting garments are much more attractive than the somewhat shapeless clothes that had been prevalent during the early Middle Ages. The clinging lines were often achieved at this time by lacing down the back, from the neck to the waist.

The working-classes were still wearing the less restricting garments, tied loosely at the waist with a leather girdle, instead of the ornate and wonderfully jewelled belts worn by the wealthy.

The two figures here represented have been taken from the tombs erected to the memory of two of Edward III's children, both of whom died in infancy. That of the boy shows us one of the very few examples of men's civil attire, as obviously the little boy was too young to be represented in armour. The elaborately dagged cloak, with its square enamelled buttons, the high collar, the golden circlet, and pointed bejewelled shoes, all show an advanced stage in fashions for this date, although it is, of course, possible that the tomb was not erected until several years after the deaths of the children.

The golden net on the head of the little princess is interesting as an early example of the emphasis of ornament in front of the ears. The long clinging lines of her cotehardie and the tight-buttoned sleeves are the earliest examples of a fashion which was to last a century or more.

I 3 2 5—I 3 5 O (*continued*)

Few indeed are the references to clothes in the contemporary records of this time, although we find
that the Scots, a wild and somewhat conservative race
regarding clothes, took exception to what they considered
effeminacy in the attire of their English enemies. Notices
were pinned up on church doors about the fashions and
manners of the English. One at St. Peter's, Stangate, was
as follows :

> " Long beards heartleffe,
> Painted hoods witleffe,
> Gay coats graceleffe
> Makes England thriftleffe ! "

The long beards must have been a fleeting fashion, as
there seems to be a scarcity of beards, either long or short,
between 1330 and 1350. Painted hoods and hats were worn
from about 1325, and embroidered and hand-painted materials
were popular throughout the century. The " gay coats "
referred to were in all probability the parti-coloured garments, a fashion which survived, in hose at least, until the
time of the Tudors.

The costume of a man of the time consisted of the following garments. Firstly the shirt, an undergarment and rarely
visible ; over this was worn the doublet, or gipon, as it
was then called. The gipon was a closely-fitting tunic
reaching to the knees, and its tightly-fitting sleeves were
usually visible under the cotehardie, or external garment.
The hose were separate, like the stockings of to-day, and
were tied to the gipon with a multitude of strings. Hoods
were worn by practically everyone ; sometimes they were
attached to cloaks, but more often were a separate garment
confining the head and shoulders, with a circular aperture
for the face.

1 3 2 5—1 3 5 0 (*continued*)

It was towards the middle of the century that English life began to recover some of its animation. Commerce and extended trade in woollen manufacture helped to enrich a nation impoverished and spiritless after a succession of long and costly wars. Prosperity had an immediate effect on costume. The somewhat meaningless draperies of the early fourteenth century took on the clinging lines associated with the costume of the Middle Ages, and dignity and grace appeared where only utility and economy had found a place.

Patterns, though simple in design, were often woven into the materials, and richly ornamented girdles and belts were worn by both men and women. Buttons of fantastic design played an important part in the decoration of gowns and cotehardies, and tassels and cords appeared on cloaks. In fact, the whole order of attire gradually took on more importance and interest.

It was during the 'thirties that the " dagged " fashion first became so popular. The term " dagged " or " jagged " means the cutting away of the edges of garments to form a pattern. Sometimes scalloped or pointed, the fashion offered great scope for individual feelings and requirements, and it soon spread to other garments, even appearing on the tops of boots and shoes. Excellent examples of " dagged " garments may be seen on the figures on contemporary tombs, although it is unfortunate that practically all the men of the period chose to have their effigies representing them in full armour. However, there are a few of children and youths and many of ladies that show, perhaps better than any other records, what beautiful lines appeared in the long dagged sleeves, and the graceful fullness of cloaks and gowns.

1 3 2 5—1 3 5 0 (*continued*)

The wimple was worn throughout the century, and the barbette, or band under the chin, which might be attached to the plaits at the side of the face or draped right round the face, was to be seen until the 'seventies. The veil and circlet, or crown, are typical of the fourteenth century. No woman's head was dressed without a veil of some description, either draped round her chin or worn over her head, or both. A gilded or jewelled circlet or an ornate net was also worn. Head-dresses constituted almost the only extravagance permitted to women at this period. While crowns or circlets were worn by the wives and daughters of noblemen, veils, nets, barbettes, and hoods were worn by all.

Women's clothes at this time fitted the figure closely to the hips and then splayed out into a wealth of graceful folds. The kirtle or under-gown was very tight-fitting, with sleeves buttoned from wrist to elbow. The surcoat worn over this was sometimes cut away at the sides in order to display a jewelled hip-belt. Occasionally the surcoat had sleeves to the elbow, and a tippet was worn. The tippet in this case was a band of contrasting material or fur, varying in length from a few inches to several feet, sewn round the arm, and allowed to hang from the elbow.

So scarce are the records of this time that, with the exception of the Loutrell Psalter and the Queen Mary Psalter, almost the only examples of English wearing apparel are to be found on tombs and wall-paintings. It is a great loss to students of contemporary fourteenth-century decoration to find that a number of valuable sources have been defaced or removed during the last hundred and fifty years. There are a few books printed at the beginning of last century which give tantalising glimpses of figures on tombs which no longer exist. Unfortunately these sketches are hardly sufficient as a basis for reliable detail.

1 3 2 5—1 3 5 0 (*continued*)

It is interesting to note that in the year 1339 Edward III received thirty thousand pounds from duties levied on the exportation of wool. The king's hold on Flanders at this time was largely due to the fact that, had this exportation ceased, half the population of the large Flemish towns would have been unemployed. Shortly after he invited Flemish weavers to take up their residence in England, and looms were set up in the eastern counties, especially Kent, and from the middle of the fourteenth century onwards woollen fabrics were woven in England.

The wealthy continued to wear silk and velvet and cloth of gold imported from abroad, but the less affluent welcomed the new woollen materials with joy and delight.

The figures on the opposite page are as typical as any of this particular twenty-five years. The hood and dagged gorget worn by the man were seen in hundreds of slightly different variations during this period, and so were the tight-sleeved kirtle, and button and tippet-trimmed surcoat worn by the woman. The veil, loosely worn over the plaited hair, was possibly the simplest method of head-dressing at this time, and certainly very charming. The simple spot pattern on her gown has been taken from a contemporary design, and if not actually woven into the material, was hand-embroidered. Some of the exquisite embroidery on the dresses of this period must have taken half a lifetime to execute, and it is fortunate in this age of leisure that by the time the embroidery was finished the gown was not too old-fashioned to wear.

1350—1375

THE difference between the attire of the ordinary people and that of the nobility was more noticeable in the men's attire than in the women's. The citizen's wife might wear a dress almost identical with one worn in the household of a knight, differing only in the apron and probably the wimple worn by the citizen's wife, and the coronet and veil and possibly the cloak worn by the knight's wife.

The vogue for embroidery spread to the homes of all, and many long hours were spent in work of this kind. Bands of simple design were to be seen at the neck and hem, and often on the sleeves, of practically all feminine attire.

The power of the Church at this time seems to have been quite negligible as regards sobriety and modesty in clothes. It is particularly interesting to note this when it is realised that priests and nuns all wore the same attire as their brothers and sisters who had not taken holy orders. The court of Edward III was singularly unhampered by the disapproval of the Church, and the extravagance and vice of the nobility was reflected in their dress.

A contemporary writer, disgusted by a recent exhibition at a tournament, gives a good description of the fashionable male attire worn during the 'sixties : " Whenever there was a tournament there came a great concourse of ladies of the most costly and beautiful, but not of the best in the kingdom, sometimes forty or fifty in number, as if they were a part of the tournament, in diverse and wonderful male apparel, in parti-coloured tunics, with short caps and bands wound round their head, and girdles bound with gold and silver, and daggers in pouches across their body . . ."

1350—1375 (*continued*)

Although it was not until the 'eighties that William Langland wrote the *Complaint of Piers Plowman*, the social conditions which he so vividly describes were very much the same as in the 'seventies, and the contrast between the poor working man and the wealthy churchman was as great.

His description of the ploughman shows how pitiful and poverty-stricken was his condition :

" His cote was of a cloute, that cary was y-called,
  His hood was full of holes, and his hair oute,
  With his knopped schon (shoes) clouted full thykke . . .
  His hosen overhangen his hokschynes, on each side . . ."

He also speaks of the friars wearing spotless linen underneath their outer garments, which were so dirty that corn might be grown in them ! The cotton cope which covered them was only an outward sign of endurance, for beneath this they were well-padded with short fur or beaver coats, and socks were surreptitiously worn inside the shoes to keep their feet from chilblains. Piers Plowman's bitterness is further increased by the fact that the clergy asking for alms in the street were often the proud possessors of six or even seven copes, and could afford the luxury of red shoes.

It was at about this time that regulations for moderation in the garments of the Grey Friars were issued : " Bredth of hood not wider than the shoulder bone, length of gown not longer than its wearer, bredth not more than sixteen spans, nor less than thirteen. The sleeves over the joint of the finger and no furthur. The mantles must be of vile and coarse cloth not curiusly made or pynched about the neck."

1375—1400

THE closing quarter of the century held the greatest changes in costume.   With the marriage of Richard II and Anne of Bohemia in 1383 the court became a centre of luxury, and the royal couple were leaders of the exaggerated fashions which prevailed.   Anne brought with her a variety of previously unknown ideas regarding clothes, the most important being the gigantic and ornate head-dresses, which were worn throughout the following century, increasing in size as the century advanced.

It was a period of fantastic costume, the beginning of the ornate and decorative attire that is always associated with the Middle Ages.   The houppelande, a gown made in a bell shape, with a hole for the neck in the centre of the circle, made its appearance during the 'eighties.   This was worn by both men and women, and was cut in varying lengths to suit the wearer.   The feminine edition was usually cut with a large aperture at the neck, and was held with a wide belt, usually embroidered, which reached from the waist to close under the breasts ; this new high waist was definitely revolutionary, and its popularity almost exceeded that of the surcoat cut away at the sides.

The masculine houppelande was high-necked, often covering the ears.   Sometimes the garment only reached the thighs, but often it fell in increasing fullness to the ankles. Houppelandes were worn right through the following century, and the gracefulness of the heavy folds was an outstanding feature of the dress of the Middle Ages.   At a later date the folds were sewn in to the waist, giving the skirt a more formal effect.

1375—1400 (*continued*)

Chaucer gives an excellent description of the houppe-lande in his picture of the friar :

> " Of double worsted was his semi-cope,
> That round was, as a belle, out of the presse."

There are many allusions to clothes in the history of this period—partly because of the new importance attached to them by the court, and partly because the people found in them an excellent opportunity for pointing a finger at the extravagance of their oppressors. John Ball, " a mad priest of Kent," as Froissart calls him, protested strongly at the wilful waste and unbridled extravagances of the rich : " They are clothed in velvets and rich stuffs, ornamented with ermine and other rich furs, while we are forced to wear poor cloth." Another interesting note is that Wat Tyler bought sixty doublets for his men at the amazingly low price of thirty marks, and incidentally never paid for them !

It was during the 'eighties that women first rode side-saddle ; previously they had all ridden astride like men, with their skirts tucked into a bag-like affair.

The toes of shoes became even more exaggerated in length than before ; the points were often tied to the knees with gold or silver chains to avoid the possibility of the wearer tripping over them.

A wealth of colourful description is to be found in Chaucer's *Canterbury Tales.* His brilliant portrayal of the numerous pilgrims leaves little to the imagination as to their appearance. Perhaps the most curious thing to us about all these descriptions is the importance placed upon the pouches, knives, and jewellery ; these etceteras obviously played a very important part in the attire of the well-dressed.

The man's hood on the opposite page is of the separate type, which was not as popular as those which enveloped the face and shoulders. His surcoat is the houppelande with the now popular bell-shaped sleeves. This type of sleeve, turned back and lined with contrasting material, and allowing the sleeves of the doublet beneath to be seen, remained in fashion throughout the following century. The jewelled girdle not only encircles the waist, but it also holds together the front of the skirts. The shoes are typical of perhaps a few years earlier ; the fashion of embroidering and bejewelling went out with the arrival of the exaggerated long-toed shoes. The girl's dress is definitely earlier than the arrival of Anne of Bohemia, probably about 1380.

1 3 7 5—1 4 0 0 (*continued*)

We read that the Wife of Bath wore scarlet hose, that the Merchant wore a " Flaundrish bever hat," and that the young Squire wore his hair curled and

> " Embroidered was he, as it were a mead
> All ful of fresshe flowers, white and red."

The ' Mellere ' wore a " Whit cote and a blew hood " ; we read of the ' Reeve ' that :

> " His beard was shave as nigh as ever he can,
> His heer was by his eres round i-shorn.
> His top was dockèd lyk a priest biforn.
> Ful longe were his legges, and ful lene,
> Al like a staff, ther was no calf y-sene.
>
> .   .   .   .   .   .
>
> A long surcote of blew uppon he hadde,
> And by his side he bar a rusty blade."

A long description of hairdressing is given in the picture of the Pardoner :

> " This pardoner had heer as yellow as wex,
> But smothe it hung, his lokkes that he hadde,
> And therwith he his shuldres overspredde.
> Full thinne it lay, in lengthes, one by one,
> And hood, for jolitte, werèd he none,
> For it was trussèd up in his wallet.
> He thought he rode al of the newe set,
> Disheveled, save his cappe, he rode all bare."

The Sergent of Lawe " rode but hoomly in a medly cote,
Girt with a girdle of silk, with barres smale ! "
And the Doctor of Phisik
> " In blue he clad was al and sangwyn
> Lynèd with taffeta and silke thin."

1 3 7 5—1 4 0 0 (continued)

There is no doubt that the works of Chaucer are, from the costume point of view, unrivalled in valuable detail. With the possible exception of some of the Diaries of the seventeenth century, no other contemporary source of any period provides us with such a wealth of interesting and valuable data as to modes and manners of the times. Not only does Chaucer describe the general appearance of his characters, but he gives also minute descriptions of materials, colours, and fashions in jewellery and hairdressing, and other interesting details which the more staid chroniclers of history fail to record.

References to some of the more exaggerated clothes of the period are to be found in several of John Wyclif's tracts. The wealthy churchmen, who paraded themselves in exaggerated sleeves, costly materials, and curled hair, was no light matter, and the delicious humour to be found in the writings of his contemporary find no place in Wyclif's writings. Little escaped Chaucer's quick eye, and he records all the minor points of detail in the Monk's costume :

> " I saw his sleves rounded at the hand
> With fur, and that the fynest in the land.
> And for to fastne his hood under his chyn
> He hadde of gold y-wrought a curious pyn :
> A love-knotte in the gretter ende ther was."

The number of references to jewellery made by Chaucer indicates what an important part it played in the costume of the period. Even the nun had her share of personal adornment :

> " Ful faire was her robe, as I was war.
> Of smal corál aboute her arme she bare
> A paire of bedes, the greatest were of grene;
> And theron hung a broch of gold ful shene,
> On which was first i-writ a crownèd A,
> And after, *Amor vincit omnia*."

1400—1420

THE manuscripts, both illuminated and illustrated, of this century, show a wealth of beautiful detail in both colour and line, but unfortunately there was no one to take Chaucer's place, and descriptions of costume are sadly lacking. As many of the manuscripts took twenty years or more to execute, it is difficult to estimate with any strict exactitude the date of the costumes illustrated, although a number of minor, if not major, changes in style over a period of twenty years help to decide within ten years or so the date of the dress.

It should be remembered, too, that the fashions at court changed slowly, and took a long time to filter down to the country, and that the garments had a long life ; thus it is possible to realise why a particular gown may be almost identical with one of fifty or sixty years earlier.

Several new styles of sleeve made their appearance at the beginning of the fifteenth century. Where previously only the tight-fitting and the bell-shaped, or a combination of the two, had been worn, there were now sleeves of practically every known shape and size. The new bagpipe sleeve, made like a gigantic bag, fitting at the shoulder and hanging in loose folds to be gathered into a tight band at the wrist, was popular for a few years. Two examples of this may be seen on the opposite page, that at the bottom being a very subdued version. The surcoat was often worn with a sleeve to the elbow, and an example of the tippet worn at the wrist of the gipon may be seen on the last figure on the page.

The tight sleeve with a roll or gathered puff at the shoulder was worn more often with the short-skirted garment. All sorts of varieties in the arrangement of the bell-shaped sleeve were to be seen ; sometimes the sleeve was turned back to the elbow, showing a fur lining ; sometimes it was gathered into a bunch at the shoulder and left to fall in deep folds under the arm. Some sleeves were so excessively long and full that the lower parts were tied in great knots to save them dragging along the ground.

I 4 0 0—I 4 2 0 (*continued*)

Variety and exaggeration in dress seem to have been general tendencies at this time; she who could outdo her neighbour in the size of head-dress and the width of skirts would deem the effort well worth while. The young squire of the day spent his all on the latest thing in embroidered surcoats and painted hoods, and went to great pains that his hair should at least be as well curled as his neighbour's. According to the miniatures of the period the hair was often crimped, giving the effect of having been tightly plaited and then undone. It is possible, however, that this was the contemporary interpretation of curly hair, and that all the young squire did was to plait his locks tightly overnight. Chaucer's Squyer, " with lokkes curled as if they lay in presse," rather gives us this impression.

The most obviously new innovation of this period was the short doublet. The hose had been cut to reach the waist, possibly as much as fifteen or twenty years earlier, and gradually the skirts of the outer garment became more and more brief, until they were eventually merely a pleated frill some six inches below the waist.

The houppelande in its most exaggerated forms, with sleeves almost as full as the gown itself sweeping the ground, was a favoured garment for those wishing to appear more dignified and prosperous than those who favoured the absurdly abbreviated tunics. Two so entirely dissimilar fashions have rarely appeared together in the history of costume.

1 4 0 0—1 4 2 0 (*continued*)

Few indeed were the garments worn at this time that were not either embroidered or patterned in some manner or other ; even when plain cloth was used it was decorated with bands of embroidery or fur. The passion for decorating even extended to the tops of hose. Tapestry-like embroideries were seen on almost every woman's gown. Embroidery had ceased to be merely a matter of spot patterns ; most of the designs were large, and were often repeated only two or three times on a garment. The designs seem to have been arranged after the garments were made, as often the central floral or imaginative motif appears on the front of a gown, with the rest of the design merely emphasising it. In smaller designs the motif appears symmetrically on the shoulders and in the middle of the back.

When spot patterns were used, they were usually larger and more dignified than those in vogue during the previous century, but their popularity waned as the century proceeded, and they made way for the boldness and exaggeration which was characteristic not only of design. Indeed, boldness and exaggeration, combined with a sense of dignity, typifies the outlook on costume during the greater part of the fifteenth century. Hardly a single fashion was introduced that was not carried to one extreme or another after it had been in vogue for a few years.

Literature had fallen to a very low level ; Chaucer was dead, and there was no one to record for posterity the life and work of the time ; indeed, almost the only literary productions were pamphlets and rhyme-sheets, and translations of French romances, which appeared in large numbers. From the point of view of costume they are quite useless, and if it were not for the letters of the Paston family it would be difficult to bridge the gap. Their letters are invaluable, and contain many details and descriptions of costumes and materials in use between 1420 and 1500.

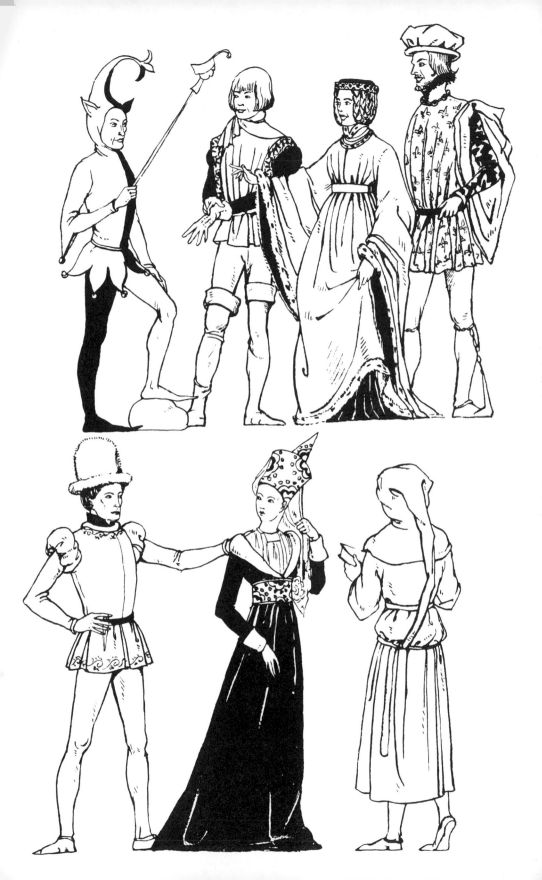

1 4 0 0—1 4 2 0 (*continued*)

Head-dresses were already tall and ornate, but they
became more and more exaggerated. The head-dress
assumed more importance, and in order that nothing should
distract attention from it, it became the fashion to pluck the
hair on the forehead and on the back of the neck. It was
a common sight to see ladies of fashion plucking their necks
in public with the aid of a small mirror or a piece of polished
metal. It was not considered any more remarkable than
it is now for a woman to be seen powdering her nose or
adding a touch of lipstick in a 'bus or drawing-room.

The illustration opposite shows the horned head-dress,
completely covered with a veil. The simple lines of the
dress are an excellent background for the amazing quantity
of fur lavished on the immense sleeves. It is interesting to
note that the man is wearing chains attached below the knee,
to which the toes of his shoes may be tied. His short gown
has the bagpipe sleeves already mentioned, and a " harness "
is slung across the shoulder. Often these " harnesses " had
bells attached. In the manuscript from which this costume
is taken the gown is white, with a bold green and pink
design ; the hat scarlet, with a gold coronet. The habit of
wearing a crown on the hat was practised a great deal by
royalty and the nobility.

I 4 0 0—I 4 2 0 (*continued*)

By 1420 the gipon was made with the high collar, and the surcoat was cut low at the neck to reveal the contrasting colour of the collar beneath. Usually the outer gown had the neck cut in a V-shape behind, and was edged with fur.

Large beaver hats, and those made of velvet and cloth, were almost as much worn as the hood, which by this time differed a great deal from its original form. The cockscomb effect was more frequently seen than previously, and the liripipe had now assumed the title of tippet. A "tippet" at this time seems to have been the name used for practically all pieces of material that were depended from the main garment.

The steeple head-dresses assumed a gigantic height during the 'twenties and 'thirties ; the veil was elongated, and was often worn over the arm to prevent it trailing the ground. It was about this time that the rather attractive eye-veil was added to this type of head-dress. The head-dress like a flower-pot on the opposite page, worn with a veil under the chin and a tie at the top, was not seen later than the 'forties. It was not nearly so popular as the steeple, horned or rolled head-dresses, examples of which are seen from the end of the fourteenth to the end of the fifteenth centuries.

It is interesting to compare the simplicity of the woman's bonnet or hood at the bottom of the page with the complicated head-dresses worn at this time. It appears to be made from a perfectly straight piece of material folded in half and sewn down the back only, the front part being cut and turned back at the face.

1420—1440

THE extravagant use of furs throughout the fifteenth century gives the impression that England was rich in animals. Much fur was imported, but it was obviously too expensive to be used profusely except by the wealthy ; the others had to content themselves with home-cured fur.

The man's gown on the page facing is cut at the sides, front, and back to facilitate riding, and is obviously lined with fur throughout. The lady's gown is richly trimmed with ermine ; the tippets on her sleeves are exaggerated into a double-skinned and voluminous drapery hanging from a band at the elbow, the end narrowing so that it may be tied round the wrist should it prove too heavy or cumbersome. It will be noticed that the box-like head attire is surmounted by a circlet of an irregular diamond shape. These circlets were also worn on top of the horned head-dress.

Shoes with extremely exaggerated toes were not so popular as they had been a few years earlier. The fashion of attaching chains to the toes of the shoes, mentioned a few pages earlier, had proved to be unsatisfactory. It was quite impracticable, and when people found it was difficult for them to walk a few steps, and impossible to walk upstairs, the craze soon died out.

The taste for fantastic clothing spread to people of all classes, which so little pleased the nobility that laws were introduced restricting those with an income of less than forty pounds a year from indulging in the most extravagant fashions. Gowns and jackets had to cover the buttocks, and the pikes on shoes were to be no longer than two feet in length !

1 4 2 0—1 4 4 0 (*continued*)

Men, as well as women, wore elaborate headgear, and their immense hats were exaggerated and ornamented to an absurd extent. The fashion for decorating the crowns of hats was first indulged in soon after the middle of the fourteenth century, but a more orthodox brim than that shown on the opposite page was then worn. Gigantic soft-crowned hats, like an electric bulb in shape, another like a three-tiered turban, and numerous other queer and exaggerated shapes, are to be seen in contemporary illustrations.

Indeed, there seems to be no limit to the variety of headdresses termed fashionable. Fringes for men were very popular at this time ; the hair was still curled and worn long, although it was often cut in a fringe all round, slanting up from the nape of the neck at the back, covering the tops of the ears at the sides, and merely an inch or so less in length on the forehead. It is curious that at a period when women tucked their hair out of sight, plucked their eyebrows, and sometimes, if we are to believe contemporary portraits, cut their eyelashes, that men should wear their hair frizzed and curled, and in elaborate fringes.

Tall, soft leather boots were worn for riding, either reaching well up the thighs or only half-way up the shins. In both cases they were turned back at the top and were often lined with a contrasting colour. Spurs were always used for riding, even on shoes and soled hose.

Although the illustrations on the opposite page do not show a variety of patterned materials, practically everything was richly embroidered, usually with large and somewhat irregular designs.

1 4 2 0—1 4 4 0 (*continued*)

The costumes depicted on the opposite page have all been specially selected to show the more sober and less exaggerated costumes worn by the older and more dignified people of the age. With the exception of the large bold designs on the materials they have little in common with the extravagant attire of the fashionable. Their somewhat sombre simplicity is in sharp contrast to the youthful and flippant garments illustrated on the previous page.

The central figure at the top of the page shows the more sober version of the horned head-dress. The horns are merely padded points over the ears, and are used as a support for the veil, which is trimmed with gathered or rouched material. Heavy gathered rouching was very fashionable for trimming, and was to be seen on even the most sober garments. Fur of all kinds was lavishly used, both for gowns and hats, and often the complete hat would be made of fur.

Small children at this time rarely wore more than a short tunic, unless they were fully clothed as miniature men and women for some very special occasion. Many examples, however, are to be seen of the very youthful page clad in an abbreviated X-shaped tunic, his long shapely legs in hose, his hair well crimped, and with a short, almost invisible, fringe peeping from beneath his flower-pot hat.

The central figure at the bottom of the page shows the method employed to fasten the hose to the gipon, when as often happened the hose were not cut to reach the waist.

The shoes illustrated are of the more useful type, some resembling a modern bedroom slipper, others consisting of a sole of leather sewn on to the hose itself.

1 4 2 0—1 4 4 0 *(continued)*

By the 'thirties head-dresses had assumed gigantic and imposing proportions. Many of these amazing conceptions can be seen on the figures on contemporary tombs, where a detailed and relief study will reveal far more than any sketch can possibly show. Both this and the colour drawing on page 59 are based on the same idea. This example, with the addition of horns beneath the coronet, makes it one of the most weird and wonderful head adornments of the time.

The surcoat worn by this lady has the sides cut away until merely a small strip of fur-edged material supports the skirt. The dark kirtle worn beneath is made almost skin-fitting in its tightness.

Both these figures show the lavishness of the extremes of fashion at this time. The man, with his curled hair, huge beaver hat, laced doublet, bunched shoulders and striped hose, was the gallant or fop of his period. Men's waists appear so small in contemporary portraits that one wonders if any form of corset was worn. Undoubtedly belts were worn much too tight to be comfortable, to give the X-shape effect which fashion demanded in the fifteenth century.

Extravagance and exaggeration are terms which occur frequently in describing the costumes of this period, and if a detailed study of social life was within the scope of this book references to greed, lust, and selfishness would appear with equal frequency in this age, when religion meant little and sorcery and magic were believed in by all. When one of the punishments for women guilty of immoral behaviour was for their hair to be cut off to the ears, and it was scandalous for women to show an inch of leg beneath their cumbersome skirts, and the Countess of Cobham did penance for practising magic, it is not difficult to imagine why Joan of Arc was condemned as a witch and a sorceress.

I 4 2 0—I 4 4 0 (*continued*)

Fantastic headgear was at its height, both literally and figuratively, during the 'thirties and 'forties of the fifteenth century.   There are so many types and varieties of absurdly exaggerated hats, especially those worn by the men, that one page of drawings is quite inadequate to give even a representative selection.   As the less fantastic fashions must have a place in this book if it is to be of any use as a general guide to the dress of the time, several of the more modest types of hoods, hats, and other head adornments have been included in the two following pages of drawings.

The large beaver and velvet hats, the dagged or jagged gorget, and tippet, and the nightcap or coif at the bottom of the page, are three examples of the more sober forms of headgear.   Headwear as an expression of personality is perhaps a limited study in these days of mass production, but in this period of the Middle Ages students of psychology would find more than enough material for study.   There seemed to be hats for every mood—fantastic or frivolous, sober or learned, and every man could let himself go in creating a model more exaggerated, more ornate, and more complicated in design than that of his neighbour.   For a few years at least the men refused to be outdone by the women in the matter of head-dress ;   even the originally simple hood was exaggerated out of all recognition, the tippet, now wide and embroidered, often trailed the ground, the gorget fell in a profusion of ornamented folds over the shoulders, and the roll or brim assumed a stiffened and enlarged appearance.

1 4 2 0—1 4 4 0 (*continued*)

The rolled head-dresses worn by the women at this time might take practically any shape. Instead of merely forming a frame for the face, as it did at first, it was now a joined affair, making a padded circle of any size to suit the wearer. Sometimes they were like a lifebelt in shape, and worn without a veil; sometimes the pad was exaggerated to a couple of yards in circumference, and bent into a variety of shapes. Heart-shapes and U-shapes were particularly popular. The front part was usually worn low on the forehead, and the sides lifted to show the fretted nets over the ears. As these rolls were often arranged eighteen inches or so above the head, it was fortunate that the architecture of the time allowed for this exaggerated height of headgear, and that the low beams of a few years later had not yet appeared.

The knobs on the head-dress of this period are particularly absurd, and it seems that if a head-dress was not considered sufficiently fantastic to please its owner, the addition of a knob on the top made amends for any other deficiency in the imagination of the wearer, if not in the eye of the beholder.

The influence of the East is very noticeable in the turban-like head-dresses worn by both men and women. The advancements and refinements of Eastern civilization were being gradually introduced to the West, and almost every European country imported silks and rugs, and exquisite pieces of workmanship, to grace the halls of the wealthy and to adorn their noble personages. The beautiful and exotic colours of the materials had a great and lasting effect on the costumes and decorations of the period to follow.

1440—1460

IN the year 1440 there is an interesting letter written by Agnes Paston to her husband, asking him to do some purchasing for her and her sister. " . . . Yil ye woulde byen her a goune, here moder Yeve ther to a godely furre. The goune nedyth for to be had ; and of colour it woulde be a godely blew, or erlys a bryghte sangueyn. I prey you de byen for me ij pypys of gold." In modern English this means that her sister wanted a gown well-trimmed with fur, either blue or bright red, and that she herself would be obliged if he would buy her two reels of gold thread for embroideries.

Colours and materials at this time were of the richest, and most brilliant ; velvets, damasks, figured satins, linen, keyrse, blanket musterdevelys, tisshew, cloth of gold, and cloth of silver, camlet, morey, frieze taffeta, and broadcloth, were materials most worn. Musterdevelys was a greyish soft woollen cloth, and was worn until about the middle of the sixteenth century ; camlet was a heavy cloth made of camel's-hair, and exceedingly expensive.

Cloth of gold was not to be worn by any one lower than a lord's estate ; neither was the use of sable permitted to any one without a title. These restrictions and others previously mentioned limiting the luxuries of dress and the extremes of fashion to certain classes seem to have been disregarded in many cases. We find, for instance, mention of two gowns of cloth of gold in the wardrobe of Sir John Falstolf in 1459.

It was during the 'forties and 'fifties of the fifteenth century that costumes reached the peak of exaggeration.

1440—1460 (*continued*)

A wealth of description of clothing is to be found in the Will of Sir John Falstolf. It is impossible to include all the details, and space can only be found for some of the more interesting data :

> " First, a gown of cloth of gold, with side sleeves surplis wise.
>
> Item 1. Another gown of cloth of gold, with straight sleeves and lined with black cloth.
>
> Item. Half a gown of red velvet.
>
> Item. Gown of blue velvet upon velvet long furred with martyns and trimmed of same, sleeves single.
>
> Item. Red gown of Lord Cornwall's livery, lined.
>
> Item. Gown cloth of green 3 yards.
>
> Item. Side scarlet gowns not lined.
>
> Item. Chammer cloak (one cut in the centre) of blue satin, trimmed with black silk."

Among his numerous jackets we find one : " The brest and slevs of blak felwett, and the remnant of russet fustian."

Some of the detailed descriptions of the hoods are extremely interesting : " Hode of blakke velvet, with a typpet half damask half velvet y-jagged." Another : " Hode of depe grene velvet, jagged upon the rolle," and another was " of russet velvet, with a typpet half of the same and half blew velvet, lined with blew damask."

There is yet another of purple velvet without roll or tippet. The tippet in this case referred to the appendage which had once been the liripipe and now hung from the roll in a profusion of folds.

The " Items " mentioned above are only a small proportion of the garments described in the Will. This gentleman owned doublets, petticoats (skirts), jackets, gowns, hoods, etc., in profusion, mostly in velvets and other rich stuffs.

1 4 4 0—1 4 6 0 (*continued*)

It will be noticed that from time to time one of the pages in each group of costumes is mainly devoted to the less exaggerated costumes of the period, and the page facing illustrates the more sober fashions of the time. It is not easy to maintain a sense of proportion ; the extremes and extravagances more readily attract the eye, and contemporary sources usually give only the more exaggerated interpretations of costume and neglect the less spectacular garments of the period.

The huge bell sleeve turned back at the wrist and showing the tight under-sleeve was worn by all classes. The figure of the boy at the bottom of the page shows an example of the detached sleeve tied at the shoulder with " points," and not attached to the gown under the arm. The sleeve of the gipon underneath is slit up to the shoulder and tied in a number of points, revealing the shirt-sleeve beneath.

The fashion for " points," a string similar to a boot-lace, was first introduced in about the 'fifties of this century. These " points " were means of tying a slashed garment where it would best display the garment worn beneath. They became even more popular in the reign of Henry VIII, and were then seen on practically every item of male attire.

It will be noticed that the examples of dress on the opposite page have little in common with those on the previous page, where an attempt has been made to indicate the elaborate decorations of fur, embroidery, and trimming on every garment. Even the veils worn on head-dresses had spangles or rouching, or ornaments of some kind, and nothing that could be decorated seemed to escape the ever-busy needles of the ladies of quality.

1440—1460 (*continued*)

In the year 1449 Margaret Paston writes to her husband, asking him to buy her some cloth, "That ye wille do byen sume frese to in maken of your child is gwnys; ye shall have best chepe and best choyse of Hayis wyf, as it is told me. And that ye wyll bye a yerd of brode clothe of blac for an hode fore me of 44d or 33d or 4 shillings a yerd for there is no good fryse in this town."

Shopping must have been a sorry business for ladies of the time. There were few shops to be found outside the big cities, and to a large extent everyone relied on pedlars. These travelling salesmen could only carry a limited stock, and if they had nothing suitable, materials for a new gown or hood had to be purchased through the services of a relative staying or living in London.

Some time in 1445 William Paston writes to his wife, asking her if she could buy some materials for his liveries. Her reply indicates how limited were the stocks kept in the smaller towns. She writes, "As touching for your liveries, there can none be got here of that colour that ye would have of, neither murrey, nor blue, nor good russets, underneath 3 shillings a yard at the lowest price, and yet is there not enough of one cloth and colour to serve you."

1 4 4 0—1 4 6 0 (*continued*)

Referring again to the invaluable Paston letters, there is a complete inventory three years later of the gowns owned by Clement Paston while at Cambridge, including " A short green gown, and a short musterdeuyllers gown. A short blue gown, a long russet gown trimmed with bever, and a long murry gown." Fur was still used a great deal, and the furs most frequently used seem to be ermine, beaver, marten, bogey, and sable.

The monstrous winged head-dress did not appear until the middle of the fifteenth century. It must have a great deal of care in laundering, and as starch was unknown at this period, some difficulty must have risen in stiffening it. Probably a solution of glue or size was used. The fashion did not last so long as the still popular steeple and roll, and comparatively few examples are to be found, although one portrait of Elizabeth Woodville shows an almost obliterated version of this butterfly effect.

1460—1480

MARGERY, the young wife of John Paston, was one of a type that has persisted through the centuries. In her letters to her husband during his absence from home there are constant references to the fact that she has " nothing to wear." In one letter she writes asking him to buy her a new gown, adding that " I have no gowne but my blak and my grene," and both of these she is tired of wearing. She also demands a girdle, as she has only one fit to wear, and her friend Elizabeth Peveral has at least fifteen or sixteen. Girdles at this time were very important items in a lady's wardrobe. They were of two main types : the wide ones, which were the only trimming to a simply-cut gown, and a narrower type jewelled and decorated for more elaborate gowns.

Girdles increased in importance and value, and a few years later, in the will of Dame Elizabeth Brown, several of different materials and design are bequeathed to various friends and relatives : " Three embroidered girdles, one tawny silk, with buckle and pendant, another purple, three of purple damask, some of ' tisshew,' some of ' red tisshew gold.' "

In 1471 John Paston writes home for some of his clothes, which he finds he requires : " Two long gowns, and two doublettes, and a jaket of plonket camlet, and a morey bonet out of my cofyr."

It will be noticed that the long gowns were nearly all split at the sides at this time. Formality in their folds was brought almost to the stage of pleats. The effect of bunched shoulders was sometimes obtained by merely catching the folds at regular intervals across the arm-hole, as in the back view at the bottom of the opposite page. The sleeve, with two openings, one at the elbow and one at the bottom of the sleeve, were worn a great deal, and as will be noticed in the coloured drawing on page 79, by slipping his hand through the lower opening the boy has given an entirely different arrangement to the sleeve.

1460—1480 (*continued*)

The charming gown worn by the lady on the opposite page is of an unusual design; the scalloped bodice and the richly embroidered skirts being of different materials. The design on the skirt is taken from a contemporary miniature. Several of these bold and beautiful designs have been the inspiration for some of the modern designs found on woollen embroideries and furnishing materials sold in most of the big London shops to-day.

The long gown worn by the man has an amusing method of adornment in the three long thin cords hanging from the yoke of the gown. They were almost invisible, and although weighted with beads, they must have got constantly tangled, and altogether been an incredible nuisance. But comfort seems to have been a secondary consideration in this century, and few garments permitted the freedom we demand to-day.

It was during the 'sixties that the fashion for short cloaks for men became prevalent. They were cut in varying lengths to reach the hem of the doublet, whether the doublet reached only the waist or continued half-way down the thighs. One or two examples of this fashion are to be found on the following pages, including a very extreme example on page 69, which barely reaches the waist. It is quite obvious that this gentleman had an income of more than forty pounds a year !

1 4 6 0—1 4 8 0 (*continued*)

The two short gowns or jackets worn by the men at the top of the page are interesting examples of new designs. The first is worn without a belt or girdle, this being unnecessary as the pleats are sewn down tightly to the waist at the back. The doublet in this case is lower in neck-line than in previous modes. The second gown is almost armour-like in its simplicity ; cut from some stiff material, it is made up without gathers or pleats of any sort, except for the slight gathering at the shoulders, which was a necessary finish to any fashionable garment in the latter part of the fifteenth century.

At the bottom of the page will be seen a new idea in boots. The boot is cut in the usual soft leather, but fits the leg so tightly that there is no drop over at the top ; the tops are cut to form a point at each side, and a design is embroidered round the edge.

A curious version of the horned head-dress appears next to the figure in boots. The hair is drawn through the horns and falls in exaggerated waves through the extreme ends of the tubes. It is extremely unusual for the hair to be seen, as at this time every wisp of hair was tucked out of sight. The sleeves are also unusual, as no less than three garments are visible ; the under-garment with tight-fitting sleeves is the smock or shift.

The use of " points " as a means of decoration can be seen in two of the figures on this page, where they are merely tied to the upper sleeve and serve no useful purpose. The small boy's hose are tied to his abbreviated gipon, and can be seen through his sideless gown. An example of the shoes worn by women can be seen on the first figure. They were made of soft leather, and with little variation were worn throughout the century. Clogs or pattens were worn by all in bad weather, and wooden soles were worn on many shoes.

1460—1480 (continued)

Another example of sewn pleats on a gown is to be seen here. The belt is merely an accessory, and does not hold the waist-line, as is usually the case. The sleeves are split right up the inside of the arm and can be worn either hanging loose, as seen here, or with the hand thrust through the fur-edged cuff at the bottom.

Soft cloth and velvet caps of absurd shapes were much worn by all men at this period.

It will be noticed that the steeple head-dresses have, by this time, assumed lappets reaching down to the shoulders on each side. This must have been the beginning of the gable head-dress worn at the beginning of the sixteenth century, an example of which may be seen on the last page of the book. The steeple itself was often decorated. A variety of patterns, of which the diamond one seen here was most popular, were used to adorn these sugar-loaf head-dresses.

Deep cuffs of a contrasting material were worn on the tight-fitting sleeves after the beginning of the 'sixties. Low-necked gowns were not often seen after this time, and when the V was cut too low to suit fashion's decree, modesties filled the gap at the front. This example has an interesting finish to the neck, as the effect of a collar is achieved without one being used. No girdle or belt is worn, the gown being cut to fit the figure closely at the waist. The fashion for wearing the kirtle pleated and fuller than the gown itself was carried on into the following century.

1 4 6 0—1 4 8 0 (*continued*)

On the opposite page may be seen the differences in the angle, height, and design of the steeple. The upper example is worn without the eye-veil, but with long exaggerated lappets decorated with jewels, and reaching well over the shoulders. The lower example is more exaggerated in height, and may be considered the extreme of the fashion. As can be seen, the hair is strained off the face, giving the head rather an egg-like appearance.

The back view next to this figure is an example of the butterfly head-dress, and shows how the ends of the material were folded and fastened at the back.

Long quills and feathers were beginning to be worn in men's hats. Pheasants' quills and others of a stiff nature were the most popular at first, but after a few years the softer types of feather took their place. These were draped round the hat or allowed to fall gracefully over the shoulder. From about 1470 until the beginning of the nineteenth century feather-trimmed hats for men never ceased to be popular.

An example of the hood worn in the original manner, but with the liripipe wound round the head and tucked in at the side, may be seen at the bottom of the page. The hood was rarely seen worn after 1465, being forsaken for caps and hats. Beaver, velvet, cloth, and wool were the most popular materials of which they were made. Even the country people preferred caps to the somewhat clumsy hoods which they had been wearing for over twenty years.

The head-dresses of the Middle Ages were gradually subsiding; the horns had gone, the ornate circlets had vanished, and soon women's head-dresses were to be referred to as " bonnets." To our modern ears this term seems quite unsuitable for the still cumbersome and ornate head-dresses.

1480—1500

THE will of Dame Elizabeth Brown, referred to a few
    pages back, includes several details of dresses which
show us how popular and important were gowns trimmed
with fur. Indeed, there seem to be few garments at this
time which were not either trimmed or lined with fur of
one sort or another : " Violet gown furred martons, black
furred with grey, black furred white, black furred martons,
a kirtle of tawny chamlet, and a purfil of ermine two skins
deep." The will also includes a piece of cloth of gold with
dropis.

A purfil was the border or trimming at the bottom of the
gown. These were obviously made separately from the
gown, and attached to any gown or kirtle as required.

The sleeves of the boy's gown on the page facing have
already been referred to. He is wearing one sleeve loose,
and he is seen putting his hand through the cuff of fur at the
bottom of the other.

The cap and hood is worn hanging down the back, with
the tippet over the shoulder to keep it in place. This was
frequently worn purely as an ornament, and another hat,
quite separate, was worn on the head.

The girdle with the pouch at the side was a very important
item of every man's attire. These pouches were almost
always decorated with embroideries, beads, or painting of
some sort. The long-toed shoes were not so popular as
they had been throughout the earlier part of the century.
They were now made almost fitting the foot, with a point
an inch or so in length. The round-toed shoe was to be the
fashionable shape for a few years before the arrival of the
absurd square-shaped shoe of the early sixteenth century.

I 4 8 O—I 5 O O (*continued*)

Although history tells us that at this period the nobles were sorely over-taxed to fill the coffers of Henry VII, the pageantry of exotic and costly gowns and garments, of a richness and extravagance hardly rivalled by the court of Elizabeth, seems to belie this. The use of gilt and silver and the lavish use of superb and wonderful furs by the nobility and wealthy merchants hardly indicates that they were taxed to the extent of impoverishment.

The visit of the Venetian ambassador to England at the end of the century is recorded. His impressions of the country are flattering, and some of his comments on the manners and modes of the late fifteenth century amusing. " They all from time immemorial wear very fine clothes, and are extremely polite in their language." Among other things, he is amazed to find that men take off their hats in the street as a salutation to each other.

Amongst the newer fashions are the striped and plain hose. The fashion for parti-coloured hose and for striped hose had been in vogue for many years, but the combination of one striped and the other plain was not introduced until about 1490. The man's short gown at the bottom of the page is cut away in front, revealing the pleated front of the doublet beneath. The different sleeves on this page will be noticed ; the one at the top on the right is lengthy, and though not nearly so full as those worn earlier, is considerably longer. The absurd little hats worn by the men at this time are in sharp contrast to the gigantic hoods worn a few years earlier.

Men wore their hair longer at this period, often allowing their curls to reach half-way down the back.

1 4 8 0—1 5 0 0 (*continued*)

It will be noticed that the outline of women's costume underwent a drastic change during the last few years of the fifteenth century. Fantastic head-dresses were no more, and the long flowing lines of the gowns of the Middle Ages gave place to the high-waisted bodices and gathered skirts of the early Tudors. The kirtle became a more important garment ; and it was often made of a richer material than the gown itself, and showed several inches below the outer skirt.

The formal drapery of the head was the beginning of the coif, which became so popular during the thirty years of the following century. But perhaps the most noticeable change in women's attire was the sleeve. For so many years the tight-fitting sleeve had been regarded as a necessary foundation for another, that the new idea of wearing a comparatively loose-fitting sleeve, revealing the wrist and sometimes the lower part of the arm, must have been readily welcomed.

One last bequest of the Paston family shows the use of at least one cosmetic—face-powder. In the year 1482, Margaret Paston leaves a purple girdle harnessed with silver and gilt to her daughter Anne. A powder box, a coarse girdle of blue harnessed with silver and gilt, and beads of silver enamelled. Also to her servant, Agnes Swan, she leaves her muster-develys gown furred with black, and a girdle of black harnessed with silver and gilt and enamelled.

The references to the ornamental belts give the impression that in the last part of the fifteenth century, at any rate, they were for the most part composed of gilt or silver, and enamelled in rich colours, rather than bejewelled.

1 4 8 0—1 5 0 0 (*continued*)

The method of ornamentation used on the sleeves of the gown worn by the man on the page facing is extremely interesting. The pattern has been cut at the edges instead of being split, which was the usual manner of displaying the shirt sleeve beneath. The points of the pattern are tied with " points " at two places. The fur-trimmed cap, the long feathers, and the long hair are all interesting innovations.

The woman's cap, with the ears enclosed in a net and a ring on the forehead, strikes a new note when accompanied by long curls at the back, and only a small black cap, instead of a gigantic one as worn a few years earlier. The simplicity of her gown still holds something of an earlier period, and the collar and cuffs and the gathered skirt show slight indications of the fashions to come.

The clothes worn during the time of the House of York show a startling difference to those worn under the Tudors, due not to the personal endeavours of Henry VII, who had little leisure for the contemplation of fashion, but to the beginnings of the intellectual revolution of the Renaissance. Although there is little to choose between the ornateness and exaggeration of both periods, the change in general outline is remarkable. The long sweeping lines of the ladies' gowns have nothing in common with the full-skirted bunchiness of the early Tudors. The square clumsy outline of the time of Henry VIII has little in common with the somewhat effeminate fussiness of the short-skirted, long-legged, be-curled gentlemen of the previous pages. Although the clothes of the fifteenth century are perhaps less enriched with costly jewels and enamels than those worn during the sixteenth century, the wonderful colours and furs are more than recompense.

I 4 8 0—I 5 oo (*continued*)

The century closes with gorgeous pageantry. Lords and ladies arrayed in cloth of gold and ermine, with girdles of exquisite and intricate design, and decked with priceless furs and jewels, and gold and silver chains worth a king's ransom, make this period more lavish than any other in the history of English Costume.

The incredibly lovely materials, with years of work in their sight-destroying embroideries, and the wonderful examples of hand-weaving, are so dignified in their design that they make the costly materials worn a century later almost vulgar in comparison. Designs of imaginary floral figures, bold and overpowering though they were, were far more effective than the tiny naturalistic interpretations worn during the time of Elizabeth.

This last page of head-dresses shows the fusing of the old and new. The gable as it was first worn is shown ; and another example was worn by widows who still clung to the wimple as a sign of mourning. The steeple at last went out of fashion about the year 1490. One or two of the ornate head-dresses of the fifteenth century were still to be seen after that date, but mostly the simpler coif and veil was favoured. Hair was to be seen once more for a few short years after a century of hiding. The small cap and long curls worn by the men show a striking contrast to the ornate, overpowering, and truly absurd erections worn on the cropped heads of fifty years earlier.

Some of the most ridiculous fashions ever worn in this country appear in this century, but they are more than balanced by some of the most charming and dignified garments ever designed to enhance the beauty of the human form.